A Speech Preparation Workbook

Third Edition

Prepared by

Suzanne Osborn

HOUGHTON MIFFLIN COMPANY   **BOSTON**   **NEW YORK**

Sponsoring Editor: Mary Finch
Development Editor: Julia Casson
Project Editor: Charline Lake
Assistant Manufacturing Coordinator: Karmen Chong
Marketing Manager: Elinor Gregory

Printed in the U.S.A.

ISBN: 0-618-53197-1

1 2 3 4 5 6 7 8 9 - EB - 08 07 06 05

Contents

Orientation to Public Speaking   1
"Other People's Words"   1
Plagiarism Questionnaire   3
Learning by Objectives Worksheet   4
Reading Log Worksheet   5

Managing Your Fear of Speaking   6
Personal Report of Communication Apprehension Scale   6
Scoring the Communication Apprehension Scale   7

Your First Speech   8
Checklist for Speech Preparation   8
Personal Awareness Inventory   9
Topic Approval Form for Speech of Self-Introduction   11
Guidelines for Preparing a Speech of Self-Introduction   13
Outline Format for Self-Introductory Speech   14
Checklist for Speech of Self-Introduction   17
Practice Presentation Feedback Form   18
Evaluation Form: Speech of Self Introduction   19

Becoming a Better Listener   21
Listening Problems Checklist   21
Speech Evaluation Form   22
Self Evaluation Form   23
Peer Evaluation Form   25
Guidelines for Evaluating an Outside Speaker   26

Adapting to Your Audience and Situation   27
Audience Analysis Questionnaire   27
Assessing Your Speech Environment   28
Assessing Your Audience   29
Value Survey I   30
Value Survey II   31
Audience Analysis Worksheet   32
Fill in the Blanks   33
Avoiding Sexist Language   34

Selecting Your Topic and Purpose   35
Personal Interest Inventory   35
Audience Interest Inventory   36
Personal/Audience Interests Worksheet   37
Topic Focusing Worksheet   38

Researching Your Speech   39

Personal Knowledge and Experience Worksheet   39
Research Strategy Worksheet   40
Research Overview Form   41
Source Credibility Questionnaire   43

Using Supporting Materials   45
Guidelines for Supporting a Point   45
Supporting a Point Worksheet   46
Checklist for Supporting a Point   47
Evaluation of One Point Presentation   48

Structuring and Outlining Your Speech   49
Worksheet for Structural Analysis   49
Guidelines for a Working Outline   51
Working Outline Worksheet   52
Checklist for a Working Outline   55
Scrambled Outline I   56
Scrambled Outline II   57

Presentation Skills   58
Checklist for Using Presentation Aids   58
Guide for Evaluating a Presentation   59
Guide for Evaluation of Voice and Articulation   60
Guide for Evaluating Impromptu Presentations   61
Evaluation Form for Question and Answer Sessions   63
Evaluation Form for Televised Presentations   65

Using Language Effectively   67
Checklist for Language Usage   67
How Much Is?   68
New Adages for Old   69

Informative Speaking   70
Checklist for Preparing an Informative Speech   70
Topic Approval Form for Informative Speech   71
What Designs to Use When   73
Informative Speech Evaluation Form   74
Guidelines for Using a Spatial Design   75
Outline Worksheet: Spatial Design   76
Checklist for a Spatial Design   79
Guidelines for Using a Sequential Design   80
Outline Worksheet: Sequential Design   81
Checklist for a Sequential Design   85
Guidelines for Using the Categorical Design   86
Outline Worksheet: Categorical Design   87
Checklist for a Categorical Design   91
Guidelines for Using a Comparative Design   92
Outline Worksheet: Comparative Design   93
Checklist for a Comparative Design   97

Contents
v

Persuasive Speaking   99
Topic Approval Form for Persuasive Speech   99
Persuasive Speech Evaluation Form   101
Guidelines for Using a Causation Design   102
Outline Worksheet: Causation Design   103
Checklist for a Causation Design   106
Guidelines for Using a Problem-Solution Design   107
Outline Worksheet: Problem-Solution Design   108
Checklist for a Problem-Solution Design   112
Guidelines for Using a Motivated Sequence Design   113
Outline Worksheet: Motivated Sequence Design   114
Checklist for a Motivated Sequence Design   117
Guidelines for Using a Refutative Design   118
Outline Worksheet: Refutative Design   119
Checklist for a Refutative Design   124
Find the Fallacy   125

Ceremonial Speaking   127
Topic Approval Form for Ceremonial Speech   127
Ceremonial Speech Evaluation Form   128
Checklist for Developing a Narrative Design   129
Outline Format for Narrative Design   130
Possible Topics for Narratives   131
Humor Orientation Scale   132

Communicating in Small Groups   133
Group Discussion Participant Evaluation Form   133
Leadership Potential Questionnaire   134
What Kind of Leader Are You?   135
What Kind of Follower Are You?   137

To the student

We have provided this *Speech Preparation Workbook* to use in your public speaking course. In this workbook you will find a variety of forms to help with preparing your self-introductory speech, analyzing your audience, selecting your topics, conducting your research, organizing supporting materials, and outlining your speeches. We have included one copy of an outline worksheet for each speech design and other materials you may need in the course. Because you may decide to use the same design for more than one assignment, make an extra copy of the blank outline worksheet so you have a backup. Make copies of other materials and forms in this workbook so that you will have enough for all of your assignments. Use these workbook materials to make your journey through the realm of public speaking a little easier to navigate.

Other People's Words

Paul Gray

Though some writers may shrug it off as the sincerest form of flattery, plagiarism is hardly a minor menace

Imagine yourself a high school history teacher who has been handed a research paper on air combat during World War II by one of your better students. In it, you come upon the following sentence, "No amount of practice could have prepared the pilot and crew for what they encountered—B-24s, glittering like mica, were popping up out of the clouds over here, over there, everywhere." A footnote identifies your student's source: *Wings of Morning* (1995), by Thomas Childers, page 83. You're conscientious about your work, so you check the reference against the Childers book, where you read, "No amount of practice could have prepared them for what they encountered. B-24s, glittering like mica, were popping up out of the clouds all over the sky."

Since it boggles the notion of probability to believe that these nearly identical sentences could have been written independently, you, dear teacher, are stuck with two possible explanations: either your student forgot the rule that the use of someone else's language must be identified as such by quotation marks— that is, that a footnote alone is not enough to indicate a word-for-word appropriation of material—or the student assumed that you wouldn't bother to track down the original passage. If you decide that sloppiness is the cause, you flunk the paper and hope the lesson will stick, this time; if you have reasons to believe that deceit was the motive, you report your student to the responsible school authorities.

But what should be the response when the malefactor isn't a teenager but rather Stephen E. Ambrose, 66, who has become over the past eight years probably the most famous and widely read historian in the United States? For, as the Weekly Standard reported in early January, Ambrose's best-selling *The Wild Blue* (2001) reproduced, footnoted but without quotation marks, the "glittering like mica" passage cited above, and two others as well, from Thomas Childers' book. Given Ambrose's prominence—he's appeared in photographs flanked by Tom Hanks and Steven Spielberg—the hunt was immediately on for other examples of apparent plagiarism in his works. Sure enough, other examples turned up: passages in *The Wild Blue* that are suspiciously similar to two other sources in addition to Childers, plus unacknowledged quotations in at least three of Ambrose's earlier books dating back to *Crazy Horse* and *Custer* in 1975.

A front page story in *The New York Times* reporting the growing furor over Ambrose's methods included a truculent mea culpa by the historian: "I wish I had put the quotation marks in, but I didn't. I am not out there stealing other people's writings. If I am writing up a passage and it is a story I want to tell and this story fits and a part of it is from other people's writing, I just type it up that way and put it in a footnote. I just want to know where the hell it came from." This explanation baffled most academic historians, not to mention most readers of it. Even those who had defended Ambrose on the grounds that the former professor—with the help of his five grown children—churns out best-selling books so rapidly that slipshod mistakes were inevitable had to reconsider. Ambrose hadn't said he'd been careless through haste, but that, by his lights, he hadn't been careless at all.

While the Ambrose story still percolated in late January, the *Weekly Standard* (yes, again) published some passages from Doris Kearns Goodwin's *The Fitzgeralds and the Kennedys* (1987) that, without quotation marks, almost exactly reproduce passages in three earlier books about the Kennedys. Asked to comment on these similarities, Goodwin, whose book on Franklin and Eleanor Roosevelt won the 1995 Pulitzer

Prize for history, told the *Weekly Standard*, " I wrote everything in longhand in those days, including the notes I took on secondary sources. . . . Drawing on my notes, I did not realize that in some cases they constituted a close paraphrase of the original work.." Yep, that is certainly one way of committing what looks like plagiarism, and it's a way that beginning students are repeatedly reminded not to take.

What, if anything, should the reading public make of the Ambrose and Goodwin dustups or of the many similar cases of plagiarism-spotting, real or fanciful, that have cropped up so often over the past few decades? Some have had real consequences. Alex Haley paid author Harold Courlander some $600,000 to settle a plagiarism suit for material Haley appropriated for *Roots* (see p. 76): Senator Joseph Biden's bid for the Democratic Presidential nomination in 1988 hit a wall when it was demonstrated that he'd lifted a stump speech, virtually verbatim, from then British Labour Party leader Neil Kinnock. Other accusations of plagiarism have dragged prominent names through headlines with inconclusive results: historian Stephen B. Oates, authors Susan Sontag and Jay McInerney. Is any of this of more than academic interest?

Certainly, if you believe that an author's words unencumbered by quotation marks have been conceived of and arranged solely by that author. This notion has been around long enough, one would think, for all concerned to have gotten the hang of it. "Original" used to mean what it still means in the term "original sin": it's not a brand-new way of being evil but a reference to the stain of mortality engendered by the illicit apple tasting in the Garden of Eden. In the preface to his *Fables, Ancient and Modern* (1700), poet John Dryden apparently struck the word's modern coinage: "I have added some original papers of my own."

That Ambrose and Goodwin have offered readers some ostensibly original sentences that are not of their own is assuredly a lapse rather than a crime. These talented, industrious historians did not plagiarize their way into eminence. But the lapses remain troubling, as do the rather blithe, dismissive self-defenses expressed by both authors. Unintentional theft remains theft, whether committed by those who know better or by those in the process of learning.

"Other People's Words," by Paul Gray, as appeared in *Smithsonian*, March, 2002. Reprinted by permission of the author.

Plagiarism Questionnaire

Read the essay "Other People's Words" and answer the following questions:

1. How does plagiarism in speaking differ from plagiarism in writing? _____

_____

_____

_____

2. Since you can't use footnotes in speeches, how can you document the sources of your information?

_____

_____

_____

3. What are the penalties for plagiarism at your school? Do you think these are too severe, too lenient, or appropriate?

_____

_____

_____

4. List five things you might do to avoid plagiarizing in your speeches

a. _____

b. _____

c. _____

d. _____

e. _____

Learning By Objectives Worksheet

Interview a specialist in your career area to investigate the importance of public speaking skills to your future work. Based on this information, prepare a list of objectives related to what you hope to gain from your public speaking class. Indicate what you might do to reach these objectives.

Name _____

Major _____

Career Aspirations _____

Person Interviewed _____

1. Objective _____

    How to reach it: _____

2. Objective _____

    How to reach it: _____

3. Objective _____

    How to reach it: _____

4. Objective _____

    How to reach it: _____

5. Objective _____

    How to reach it: _____

READING LOG

As you read the materials assigned in this course, keep a log of what you are learning. Look for creative applications of the ideas you are reading about in terms of their applicability to the current assignment and their applicability outside of class. Make additional copies of this form to use on all your reading assignments.

Name: _____

Date: _____

Title (or text chapter):_____

Author (if not from text): _____

Source (if not from text): _____

Applicability to current assignment:_____

_____

_____

_____

_____

_____

Applicability outside of class:_____

_____

_____

_____

_____

_____

_____

Personal Report of Communication Apprehension Scale*

Directions: This instrument is composed of 20 statements concerning your feelings about communication with other people. Please indicate in the space provided the degree to which each statement applies to you by marking whether you:

1 = Strongly Agree
2 = Agree
3 = Are Undecided
4 = Disagree
5 = Strongly Disagree

There are no right or wrong answers. Many of the statements are similar to other statements. Do not be concerned about this. Work quickly; just record your first impressions.

_____ 1. When participating in a meeting with people I don't know well, I feel very nervous.

_____ 2. I have no fear of facing an audience.

_____ 3. I look forward to expressing my opinions at meetings..

_____ 4. I look forward to an opportunity to speak in public.

_____ 5. I find the prospect of speaking somewhat pleasant.

_____ 6. When speaking in public my posture feels strained and unnatural.

_____ 7. I am tense and nervous while participating in group discussions.

_____ 8. Although I talk fluently with friends, I am at a loss for words before an audience.

_____ 9. My hands tremble when I try to handle objects during a presentation.

_____ 10. I always avoid speaking in public if possible.

_____ 11. I feel that I am more fluent when talking in meetings than most other people are.

_____ 12. I am fearful and tense all the while I am speaking before a group of people.

_____ 13. My thoughts become confused and jumbled when I speak before an audience.

_____ 14. Although I am nervous just before getting up, I soon forget my fears and enjoy the
            experience.

_____ 15. Talking to people who hold positions of authority makes me fearful and tense.

_____ 16. I dislike using my voice and body expressively.

_____ 17. I feel relaxed and comfortable while speaking.

_____ 18. I feel self-conscious when I am called upon to answer a question or give an opinion in class.

_____ 19. I face the prospect of making a speech with complete confidence..

_____ 20. I would enjoy presenting a speech on a local television show.

---

* Adapted from James C. McCroskey, <u>An Introduction to Rhetorical Communication,</u> 6th ed. (Englewood Cliffs, NJ: Prentice Hall) 1993, p. 37-39.

Scoring the Communication Apprehension Scale

Scoring

(1) Add the responses for the following questions to obtain the N score:

$$N = 1 + 6 + 7 + 8 + 9 + 10 + 12 + 13 + 15 + 16 + 18$$

(2) Add the responses for the following questions to obtain the P score:

$$P = 2 + 3 + 4 + 5 + 11 + 14 + 17 + 19 + 20$$

(3) Substitute the N and P scores in the following formula to determine your total score:

$$CA = (66 - N) + P$$

Descriptive Statistics

Range:	20 - 100
Mean:	50.45
Standard deviation:	11.58
Internal reliability:	.93
Excessive apprehension:	62 and higher

If you score above 55 on this scale, consult with your instructor for help with your problem.

Checklist for Speech Preparation

_____   Analyze your audience and speaking situation.

_____   Select your topic: focus on something that can be handled within the time constraints of your assignment and the time needed for preparation.

_____   Determine your purpose for speaking. Think clearly about what you want to accomplish with your presentation.

_____   Review your purpose in terms of how it fits with your specific audience and speaking situation.

_____   Reconsider your topic selection in light of audience and situational factors and your purpose for speaking.

_____   Begin researching your topic. If necessary, refocus your topic and adjust your purpose in light of your research.

_____   Develop a preliminary outline of the body of your speech.

_____   Check the adequacy of your research in terms of responsible knowledge and sufficient supporting material. Do additional research as needed.

_____   Check the organization of your main ideas. Do they flow smoothly? Is the speech easy to follow?

_____   Adapt your preliminary outline to reflect needed changes.

_____   Develop your preliminary outline of the body of your speech into a formal outline format.

_____   Write an introduction for your speech.

_____   Develop a conclusion for your speech.

_____   Prepare a key-word outline to use for cues during your presentation.

_____   Practice your presentation.

Personal Awareness Inventory

1. What factors in my cultural background have influenced me the most?

_____

_____

_____

_____

2. What factors in my environment have influenced me the most?

_____

_____

_____

_____

3. What person or persons have had a real impact on my life?

_____

_____

_____

_____

_____

4. What experiences have I had that have shaped me as a person?

_____

_____

_____

_____

_____

5. What activities of mine define me as a person?

_____

_____

_____

_____

6. What type of influence has my work had in shaping me?

_____

_____

_____

_____

7. Do I have a goal or purpose in life that shapes my behavior?

_____

_____

_____

_____

8. Do I have special values that influence my life?

_____

_____

_____

_____

Topic Approval Form for a Speech of Self-Introduction

Name: _____

Instructor: _____

Class Meeting Time: _____

Present two topic ideas for your speech of self-introduction. Write out the message you want the audience to get from your speech and what effect this might have on your ethos for future informative and persuasive speeches. Indicate which topic idea you would be most interested in developing.

Topic: _____

Message: _____

_____

_____

Ethos Development: _____

_____

_____

* * * * * * * *

Topic: _____

Message: _____

_____

_____

Ethos Development: _____

_____

Guidelines for Preparing a Speech of Self-Introduction

The speech of self-introduction provides you with an opportunity to develop credibility before your audience. It is a chance for you to be seen as competent, trustworthy, likeable, and forceful. Since no one can relate his or her life story in a single speech, you should choose a topic that best defines you (or the person you are introducing). Use the Self-Awareness Inventory on pp. 9-10 to help you come up with a specific topic for your presentation. Write down responses to all of the questions in the inventory, then think through all of these potential topic areas before making a decision on your topic.

Once you have determined your topic, begin to plan your speech. Be certain that it has an introduction, body, and conclusion. Start by planning the body of your speech. In the body of your speech you will develop your major ideas (main points). You may include up to three main points in your presentation. Each main point must be supported by facts and figures, examples, or narratives. These materials should be inserted into the outline worksheet in the appropriate places.

After you have prepared the body of your speech you should develop an introduction that grabs audience attention and leads into the body of your speech. Finally you should prepare a conclusion that summarizes your message and concluding remarks that reflect on the meaning and significance of your speech.

Outline Format for Self-Introductory Speech

Introduction

    I. Attention-arousing and orienting material_____

_____

_____

    II. Preview:_____

_____

_____

Body

    I. Main point #1: _____

_____

        Supporting Material: _____

_____

_____

_____

    II. Main point #2:_____

_____

        Supporting Material: _____

_____

_____

_____

    III. Main point #3: _____

_____

Supporting Material: _____

_____

_____

_____

Conclusion

I. Summary Statement: _____

_____

_____

II. Concluding Remarks: _____

_____

_____

_____

Checklist for a Speech of Self-Introduction

_____   I narrowed my topic to the one thing that best defines me as an individual.

_____   My introduction creates attention and interest.

_____   My introduction previews the main point(s) of my speech.

_____   The body of my speech contains 1, 2, or 3 main points.

_____   Each main point of my speech is supported by either facts and figures, examples, or narratives.

_____   My conclusion contains a summary that recaps my message.

_____   I end my speech with concluding remarks that leave the audience with something to remember.

Practice Presentation Feedback Form

Practice presenting your speech before a classmate. Have your classmate complete this feedback form to help you refine your speech.

1. Did the introduction gain your attention? What other techniques might the speaker want to consider?

2. Did the introduction adequately preview the speech? Would such a preview be desirable or necessary?

3. Was the purpose of the speech clear? What was it?

4. Could you pick out the main points of the speech? What were they?

5. Was there sufficient supporting material? Were examples or narratives interesting?

6. Did the conclusion effectively summarize the message?

7. Did the concluding remarks leave you with something to remember?

8. Did the presentation sound natural and spontaneous?

9. What specific advice would you offer the speaker?

Evaluation Form
Self-Introductory Speech

Name _____ **Date** _____ **Topic** _____

General

_____ Did the speaker seem committed to the topic?

_____ Did the speech fulfill the specifics of assignment?

_____ Did the speech promote identification among topic, audience, and speaker?

_____ Was purpose of the speech clear?

_____ Was the topic handled with imagination and freshness?

_____ Did the speech meet high ethical standards?

Substance and Structure

_____ Did the introduction arouse interest?

_____ Was the speech easy to follow?

_____ Could you identify the main points of the speech?

_____ Were main ideas supported by examples or narratives?

_____ Did the conclusion help you remember the speech?

Presentation

_____ Was the language clear, simple, and direct?

_____ Was the language colorful?

_____ Were grammar and pronunciations correct?

_____ Was the speech presented extemporaneously?

_____ Were notes used unobtrusively?

_____ Was the speech presented enthusiastically?

_____ Did the speaker maintain good eye contact?

_____ Did the presentation sound "conversational"?

Comments:

Grade _____

Listening problems checklist

_____ 1. I believe listening is an automatic process, not a learned behavior.

_____ 2. I stop listening and think about something else when a speech is uninteresting.

_____ 3. I find it hard to listen to speeches on topics about which I feel strongly.

_____ 4. I react emotionally to trigger words.

_____ 5. I am easily distracted by noises when someone is speaking.

_____ 6. I don't like to listen to speakers who are not experts.

_____ 7. I find some people too objectionable to listen to.

_____ 8. I nod off when someone talks in a monotone.

_____ 9. I can be so dazzled by a glib presentation that I don't really listen to the speaker.

_____ 10. I don't like to listen to speeches that contradict my values.

_____ 11. I think up counterarguments when I disagree with a speaker's perspective.

_____ 12. I know so much on some topics that I can't learn from most speakers.

_____ 13. I believe the speaker is the one responsible for effective communication.

_____ 14. I find it hard to listen when I have a lot on my mind.

_____ 15. I stop listening when a subject is difficult.

_____ 16. I can look like I'm listening when I am not.

_____ 17. I listen only for facts and ignore the rest of a message.

_____ 18. I try to write down everything a lecturer says.

_____ 19. I let a speaker's appearance determine how well I listen.

_____ 20. I often jump to conclusions before I have listened all the way through a message.

Speech Evaluation Form

SPEAKER_____ TOPIC_____ DATE_____

Overall Considerations

_____ Did the speaker seem committed to the topic?
_____ Did the speech meet the requirements of the assignment?
_____ Was the speech adapted to fit the audience?
_____ Did the speech promote identification among topic, audience, and speaker?
_____ Was the purpose of the speech clear?
_____ Was the topic handled with imagination and freshness?
_____ Did the speech meet high ethical standards?

Substance

_____ Was the topic worthwhile?
_____ Had the speaker done sufficient research?
_____ Were the main ideas supported with reliable and relevant information?
_____ Was testimony used appropriately?
_____ Were the sources documented appropriately?
_____ Were examples or narratives used effectively?
_____ Was the reasoning clear and correct?

Structure

_____ Did the introduction spark your interest?
_____ Did the introduction adequately preview the message?
_____ Was the speech easy to follow?
_____ Could you identify the main points of the speech?
_____ Were transitions used to tie the speech together?
_____ Did the conclusion summarize the message?
_____ Did the conclusion help you remember the speech?

Presentation

_____ Was the language clear, simple and direct?
_____ Was the language colorful?
_____ Were grammar and pronunciations correct?
_____ Was the speech presented extemporaneously?
_____ Were notes used unobtrusively?
_____ Was the speaker appropriately enthusiastic?
_____ Did the speaker maintain good eye contact?
_____ Did gestures and body language complement ideas?
_____ Was the speaker's voice expressive?
_____ Were the rate and loudness appropriate to the material?
_____ Did the speaker uses pauses appropriately?
_____ Did visual aids make the message clearer or more memorable?
_____ Were visual aids skillfully integrated into the speech?
_____ Was the presentation free from distracting mannerisms?

Becoming a Better Listener

Self-Evaluation Form

Name _____ Date _____

Topic _____

Strengths of this assignment: _____

                                                     _____

  _____

  _____

  _____

Areas I need to work on: _____

  _____

  _____

  _____

Grade I deserve _____

* *

Instructor's Evaluation:

Grade:

Peer Evaluation Form

Speaker _____ Topic _____Date _____

Introduction:

1. Did the introduction gain your attention? How?_____

    _____

2. Did the speaker establish credibility to speak on the topic? How?_____

    _____

3. Did the speaker adequately preview the main points?_____

Body:

1. Was the speech easy for you to follow? _____ Identify the main points:

    (1) _____

    (2) _____

    (3) _____

2. Were the main points arranged effectively? _____ What type of design was used?_____

    _____ Might a different design have been better? _____ What design

    would you suggest?_____

3. Was supporting material sufficient and appropriate? _____ Please comment: _____

    _____

4. Did you find the speech interesting? _____ Why or Why not? _____

    _____

Conclusion:

1. Did the speaker summarize the message? _____

2. Did you feel the speech was complete?_____

3. Were you left with something to remember? _____ What? _____

    _____

Suggestions for Improvement (Please note two things the speaker could do to improve his/her next

presentation):

1. _____

2. _____

Guidelines for Evaluating an Outside Speaker

1. How would you rate the speaker's ethos?

2. Was the speech well adapted to the audience's needs and interests?

3. Did the speech take into account the cultural complexity of its audience?

4. Was the speech attuned to audience values?

5. Was the message clear?

6. Was the message well structured?

7. Was language used effectively?

8. Was the speech skillfully presented?

9. How did listeners respond, both during and after the speech?

10. Did the communication environment have an impact on the message?

11. Did the speech achieve its goals?

12. Was the speech ethical in terms of responsible knowledge and the use of communication techniques?

Audience Analysis Questionnaire

Sex: M F Age _____ Academic Year: FR SO JR SR GPA _____ Race_____

Marital status _____ Religious preference _____

Major _____ State lived in longest _____

Current job: (full or part-time) _____ Hours per week _____

Career aspirations: _____

Persons I admire most: (Male) _____ (Female) _____

Political preferences :   [liberal, conservative, moderate]   [Democrat, Republican, other]
                                    (circle one)   (circle one)

Group memberships (occupational, political, religious, or social)_____

_____

Father's occupation _____ Mother's occupation _____

Place of birth _____ Places lived _____

Travel (in USA) _____

Travel (outside USA) _____

Hobbies _____

_____

Positive "trigger words" _____

Negative "trigger words" _____

The most important thing in my life right now is _____

_____

Topics on which I would like to hear an informative speech (name 3) _____

_____

Topics on which I would like to hear a persuasive speech (name 3) _____

_____

Assessing Your Speech Environment

1. Should you anticipate any problems with your presentation due to time or timing?

2. What should you consider about the physical setting where you will be speaking? How might the size of the room or the availability of special equipment effect your presentation?

3. How might audience expectations for this particular occasion effect your presentation?

4. Is there any late-breaking news that might effect the way your audience perceives your topic?

5. Is there a good chance that other speakers might address this topic before you? If so, how would you adjust to it?

6. How large and diverse is your audience? Who is your primary audience? How might this relate to your preparation and presentation?

Assessing Your Audience

1. What beliefs, attitudes, needs, interests, or values do you share with the members of your primary audience? How might you build on this common ground to support your thesis?

2. What audience demographics (age, gender, education level, group & political affiliations, religion, socio-cultural background) might be relevant to your topic and purpose/thesis statements? Can your audience be characterized in respect to predominate demographic characteristics?

3. How important is your topic to your audience? Do they already care about it? Why? If not, how can you motivate them to listen?

4. What aspects of your topic will be most relevant to them? How might you best gain and hold their attention from the beginning of your speech?

5. What do they already know about your topic? What do they want and need to know in order to establish your main points and assertions responsibly?

6. How do they feel about your topic? Would they be predisposed to act in a positive, neutral, or negative fashion? Can you think of any obvious reasons why they may not be open to your proposal or any other new ideas in respect to your topic and purpose?

Value Survey I

On this page are 18 values listed in alphabetical order. Your task is to arrange them in the order of their importance to YOU. Study the list carefully and pick out the one value which is the most important for you. Write the letter of that value on the line next to number 1. Then pick out the value that is second most important and write the letter of that value on the line next to number 2.

Continue to do the same for each of the remaining values. The value which is least important to you goes on the line next to number 18.

1. _____   A. A comfortable life

2. _____   B. An exciting life

3. _____   C. A sense of accomplishment

4. _____   D. A world at peace

5. _____   E. A world of beauty

6. _____   F. Equality

7. _____   G. Family security

8. _____   H. Freedom

9. _____   I. Happiness

10. _____   J. Inner harmony

11. _____   K. Mature love

12. _____   L. National security

13. _____   M. Pleasure

14. _____   N. Salvation

15. _____   O. Self-respect

16. _____   P. Social recognition

17. _____   Q. True friendship

18. _____   R. Wisdom

money

Fame

Value Survey II

On this page are 18 values listed in alphabetical order. Your task is to arrange them in the order of their importance to YOU. Study the list carefully and pick out the one value which is the most important for you. Write the letter of that value on the line next to number 1. Then pick out the value that is second most important and write the letter of that value on the line next to number 2. Continue to do the same for each of the remaining values. The value which is least important to you goes on the line next to number 18.

1. _____   A. Ambitious

2. _____   B. Broadminded

3. _____   C. Capable

4. _____   D. Cheerful

5. _____   E. Clean

6. _____   F. Courageous

7. _____   G. Forgiving

8. _____   H. Helpful

9. _____   I. Honest

10. _____   J. Imaginative

11. _____   K. Independent

12. _____   L. Intellectual

13. _____   M. Logical

14. _____   N. Loving

15. _____   O. Obedient

16. _____   P. Polite

17. _____   Q. Responsible

18. _____   R. Self-controlled

Audience Analysis Worksheet

Topic_____

Audience_____

Factor description   **Adaptations needed**

Time: _____   _____

Place: _____   _____

Occasion: _____   _____

Audience size: _____   _____

Context: _____   _____

Age: _____   _____

Gender: _____   _____

Education: _____   _____

_____   _____

Group affiliations: _____   _____

_____   _____

Sociocultural background: _____   _____

_____   _____

Interest in Topic: _____   _____

_____   _____

Knowledge of Topic: _____   _____

_____   _____

Attitude regarding topic: _____   _____

_____   _____

Values regarding topic_____   _____

_____   _____

_____   _____

Motivational Appeals _____   _____

_____   _____

Fill in the Blanks:

1. After a hard day on the job, the secretary _____

   _____

2. When the plumber arrived at my house _____

   _____

3. The doctor was most helpful with my problems, in fact _____

   _____

4. My child's teacher is outstanding, for example _____

   _____

5. When a basketball player graduates from college _____

   _____

6. On the tour the President was accompanied by _____

   _____

7. While I was in the hospital I had the most wonderful nurse, in fact _____

   _____

8. When the construction supervisor arrived at the scene of the accident _____

   _____

Avoiding sexist language

What alternatives can you suggest for the following words?

Early man   _____

Mankind   _____

Mailman   _____

Manmade   _____

Congressman   _____

Chairman   _____

Repairman   _____

Businessman   _____

Manpower   _____

Personal Interest Inventory

Places   **People**   **Activities**

_____   _____   _____

_____   _____   _____

_____   _____   _____

_____   _____   _____

_____   _____   _____

Objects   **Events**   **Goals**

_____   _____   _____

_____   _____   _____

_____   _____   _____

_____   _____   _____

_____   _____   _____

Values   **Problems**   **Campus Concerns**

_____   _____   _____

_____   _____   _____

_____   _____   _____

_____   _____   _____

_____   _____   _____

Audience Interest Inventory

Places   **People**   **Activities**

_____   _____   _____

_____   _____   _____

_____   _____   _____

_____   _____   _____

_____   _____   _____

Objects   **Events**   **Goals**

_____   _____   _____

_____   _____   _____

_____   _____   _____

_____   _____   _____

_____   _____   _____

Values   **Problems**   **Campus Concerns**

_____   _____   _____

_____   _____   _____

_____   _____   _____

_____   _____   _____

_____   _____   _____

Personal and Audience Interests Worksheet

Personal Interests	Audience Interests	Potential Topics
_____	_____	_____
_____	_____	_____
_____	_____	_____
_____	_____	_____
_____	_____	_____
_____	_____	_____

Topic Focusing Worksheet

Who
_____
_____
_____

What
_____
_____
_____

When
_____
_____
_____

Where
_____
_____
_____

Why
_____
_____
_____

How
_____
_____
_____

Personal Knowledge and Experience Worksheet

What I Know	Where/how I learned it	What I need to find out
_____	_____	_____
_____	_____	_____
_____	_____	_____
_____	_____	_____
_____	_____	_____
_____	_____	_____

Examples/Narratives I might use:

_____

_____

_____

_____

_____

_____

Research Strategy Worksheet

Topic:_____

Specific purpose:_____

General information source: (list a source of general information applicable to your topic)

_____

Key terms and access to information sources: (list the key terms you will use and 2 sources of access to information you will use to identify specific and/or in-depth references)

Key terms   1. _____   2. _____

Access   1. _____   2. _____

Specific and/or in-depth information references: (list 3 or 4 references to specific and/or in-depth information applicable to your topic of which at least 2 must be from periodicals or books)

1._____

_____

2._____

_____

3._____

_____

4._____

_____

Current information references: (list 1 or 2 sources of current information if applicable to your topic)

1._____

_____

2._____

_____

Local applications sources: (list 1 or 2 sources for local applications material if applicable to your topic)

1._____

_____

2._____

_____

Research Overview Form
(page 1)

Source: Main Points:

_____   _____

_____   _____

_____   _____

                                           _____

                                           _____

Source: Main Points:

_____   _____

_____   _____

_____   _____

                                           _____

                                           _____

Source: Main Points:

_____   _____

_____   _____

_____   _____

                                           _____

                                           _____

Research Overview Form
(page 2)

Source: Main Points:

_____   _____

_____   _____

_____   _____

                                                 _____

                                                 _____

Source: Main Points:

_____   _____

_____   _____

_____   _____

                                                 _____

                                                 _____

Source: Main Points:

_____   _____

_____   _____

_____   _____

                                                 _____

                                                 _____

SOURCE CREDIBILITY QUESTIONNAIRE

Students use a variety of sources in preparing classroom speeches. These sources may range from highly credible to barely believable. A highly credible source is one that is seen as **accurate, unbiased, trustworthy,** and **fair**.

The following is a list of sources frequently used in student speeches. Please indicate how credible you believe each source is using the following scale:

> 5 = very high credibility
> 4 = high credibility
> 3 = average credibility
> 2 = low credibility
> 1 = very low credibility
> N = not familiar with this publication

Please circle the appropriate number that represents your estimate of the credibility of each of the following publications:

Publication	5	4	3	2	1	N
Time Magazine	5	4	3	2	1	N
Cosmopolitan	5	4	3	2	1	N
Changing Times	5	4	3	2	1	N
The New Yorker	5	4	3	2	1	N
Esquire	5	4	3	2	1	N
Today's Health (AMA)	5	4	3	2	1	N
Wall Street Journal	5	4	3	2	1	N
National Geographic	5	4	3	2	1	N
Reader's Digest	5	4	3	2	1	N
U.S. News and World Report	5	4	3	2	1	N
Sports Illustrated	5	4	3	2	1	N
Ladies' Home Journal	5	4	3	2	1	N
New England Journal of Medicine	5	4	3	2	1	N
National Inquirer	5	4	3	2	1	N
New York Times	5	4	3	2	1	N
People	5	4	3	2	1	N
Playboy	5	4	3	2	1	N
Newsweek	5	4	3	2	1	N
Psychology Today	5	4	3	2	1	N
Ms	5	4	3	2	1	N
TV Guide	5	4	3	2	1	N
Harvard Business Review	5	4	3	2	1	N
Field and Stream	5	4	3	2	1	N
Ebony	5	4	3	2	1	N
Popular Mechanics	5	4	3	2	1	N
The American Psychologist	5	4	3	2	1	N
Money	5	4	3	2	1	N
Rolling Stone	5	4	3	2	1	N
USA Today	5	4	3	2	1	N

AGE _____ SEX _____ RACE _____ CLASSIFICATION: Sr Jr Soph Fresh Other

Guidelines for Supporting a Point

This is an exercise to help you learn how to use supporting materials effectively in your speeches. It provides you with an opportunity to make a relatively simple presentation to your audience. The research you need to do for this presentation and the time it should take you to organize and prepare it is minimal.

Begin by deciding on a statement, claim, or assertion that would need to be supported before listeners would accept it. Write this in the proper place in your worksheet. Go to the library to research the statement you wish to support. Look for facts and information that support your statement. Facts are verifiable units of information and should come from sources the audience respects. Your information should be relevant to your claim and should represent the most recent facts on the topic. Put this information in the proper place on your outline worksheet. After you have entered your factual information, find some testimony that supports your statement and include it in the appropriate space on the worksheet. You should use expert testimony from a source who is competent to speak on the subject. Next, find an example or narrative that further demonstrates your point. Enter this material in the appropriate space on the worksheet.

Once you have decided on the facts and figures, testimony, and narrative examples you will use to support your point, you should plan transitions so that your presentation flows smoothly. You should have transitions between the statement and supporting materials, between the different types of supporting materials, and between the supporting materials and the restatement of your original assertion. Prepare these transitions and insert them into the worksheet in the appropriate places.

Supporting a Point Worksheet

Statement: _____

Transition into facts or statistics: _____

_____

    1. Factual information or statistics to support statement: _____

_____

_____

Transition into testimony: _____

_____

    2. Testimony to support statement: _____

_____

_____

_____

Transition into example or narrative: _____

_____

    3. Example or narrative to support statement: _____

_____

_____

_____

Transition into restatement: _____

_____

Restatement: _____

Works Cited:

Checklist for Supporting a Point

_____ I have selected a claim or assertion that needs to be supported to be accepted by my audience.

_____ I have selected facts and figures from a credible, unbiased source of information.

_____ I have identified the source(s) of my information.

_____ I have found expert testimony to support my claim or assertion.

_____ I have introduced the source of testimony and established his or her credentials to speak on the topic.

_____ I have developed an example or narrative that focuses attention on the most important aspect of my claim or assertion.

_____ I have planned transitions to make my presentation flow smoothly.

_____ I have prepared a list of works consulted that contains at least two references, only one of which is from an encyclopedia or dictionary.

Evaluation of One-Point Presentation

NAME _____ SECTION _____ GRADE _____

Factual information or statistics:

Relevance to point	5	4	3	2	1
Recency of information/statistics	5	4	3	2	1
Source/date identified	5	4	3	2	1
Credibility of source	5	4	3	2	1
Freedom from distortion	5	4	3	2	1
Facts rather than opinions	5	4	3	2	1

Testimony:

Relevance to point	5	4	3	2	1
Recency of testimony	5	4	3	2	1
Proper type of testimony used	5	4	3	2	1
Qualifications specified	5	4	3	2	1
Accuracy of quote or paraphrase	5	4	3	2	1

Example or Narrative:

Relevance to point	5	4	3	2	1
Representative of situation	5	4	3	2	1
Plausibility	5	4	3	2	1
Interest value	5	4	3	2	1

General:

Use of transitions to integrate	5	4	3	2	1
Extemporaneous presentation	5	4	3	2	1

Comments:

Worksheet for Structural Analysis

Use this worksheet to analyze the structure of one of the speeches contained in your text.

Introduction:

Attention material _____

Establishment of ethos _____

Preview or transition _____

Length (in relation to body and conclusion) _____

Body:

Main Point #1 _____

     Type and amount of support _____

     Transition to point #2 _____

     Length (relative to other main points) _____

Main Point #2 _____

     Type and amount of support _____

     Transition to point #3 _____

     Length (relative to other main points)_____

     Main Point #3 _____

     Type and amount of support _____

     Transition to conclusion _____

     Length (relative to other main points)_____

Conclusion:

     Summary of message _____

     Concluding material _____

     Length (in relation to body and introduction)_____

Guidelines for a Working Outline

A working outline helps you organize and develop your speech. It is a tentative plan that shows you how your ideas are evolving, whether they fit together, and if you have enough supporting materials.

This program prompts you to organize and reorganize your material as you work toward the formal outline of your speech. You can make revisions without having to rewrite or retype your entire outline. You can use the worksheet to rearrange your material as needed. By making, saving, and printing out several versions of your working outline, you can refine the structure of your speech.

Start your working outline by listing your topic, specific purpose, and thesis statement. Keep these clearly in mind as you plan the body of your speech. Identify the main ideas (your main points) from your research. For each main point, determine the major subdivisions (subpoints) of the material. In later working outlines you may also identify sub-sub points for each subpoint.

After you have identified your main points and subpoints, develop an introduction that fits the body of your speech. Your introduction should contain material that gains attention, establishes your credibility, and previews your message. Next, you should prepare a conclusion that includes a summary and concluding remarks. Finally, you should prepare transitions for use between the introduction and body, each main point, and the body and conclusion of your speech.

As you revise your working outline, be sure to revise your preview and summary statements to reflect the changes you make. As you save different versions of your working outline, you may wish to save them as "Working Outline 1, computers," "Working Outline 2, computers."

Working Outline Worksheet

Title: _____

Topic: _____

Specific Purpose:_____

_____

Thesis Statement:_____

_____

Introduction

Attention Material: _____

_____

Credibility Material: _____

_____

Preview:_____

_____

[Transition to body of speech]

_____

Body

Main point I:_____

_____

    Subpoint A: _____

_____

_____

    Subpoint B: _____

_____

_____

[Transition to body of speech]

_____

Main point II: _____

    Subpoint A: _____

    _____

    _____

    Subpoint B: _____

    _____

    _____

[Transition to next main point]

_____

Main point III: _____

_____

    Subpoint A: _____

    _____

    _____

    Subpoint B: _____

    _____

    _____

[Transition to next main point]

_____

Main point IV: _____

_____

    Subpoint A: _____

    _____

    _____

Subpoint B: _____

_____

_____

[Transition to next main point]

_____

Main point V:_____

_____

Subpoint A: _____

_____

_____

Subpoint B: _____

_____

_____

[Transition to conclusion]

_____

Conclusion

Summary: _____

_____

Concluding remarks: _____

_____

_____

Checklist for a Working Outline

_____ 1. My topic, specific purpose, and thesis statement are clearly stated.

_____ 2. I have listed the most important ideas about my topic as main points.

_____ 3. I have no more than five main points.

_____ 4. Each subpoint breaks its main point into more specific detail.

_____ 5. My introduction contains attention-getting material, establishes my credibility, and previews my message.

_____ 6. I have prepared transitions to use between the introduction and body, between each main point, and between the body and conclusion of my speech.

_____ 7. I have revised my specific purpose, thesis statement, and preview as needed to reflect any changes in my working outline.

_____ 8. I have made several revisions of my working outline to be sure my speech is well organized.

Scrambled Outline I

The following material is an outline in format only. Rearrange it so that it follows the conventions of coordination and subordination. Be sure that each point relates directly to the point that precedes it.

Thesis statement: Deer hunting with a camera can be an exciting sport.

I.   There is a profound quiet, a sense of mystery.
    A. The woods in the late fall are enchanting
       1. The film-hunter becomes part of a beautiful scene.
       2. Dawn is especially lovely.
    B. Time that a big doe walked under my tree stand.
       1. When they appear, deer always surprise you.
       2. How a big buck surprised me after a long stalk.

II.   Hunting from a stand can be a good way to capture a deer on film.
    A. The stalk method on the ground is another way to hunt with a camera.
       1. Learn to recognize deer tracks and droppings.
          a. Learn to recognize deer signs.
          b. Learn to recognize rubs on trees and scrapes on the ground.
       2. Hunt into the wind and move slowly.
    B. There are two main ways to hunt with a camera.
       1. Stands offer elevation above the line of sight.
       2. Portable stands are also available.
       3. Locating and building your permanent stand.

III.   The right camera can be no more expensive than a rifle.
    A. Selecting the right camera for film-hunting is essential.
    B. Certain features—like a zoom lens—are necessary.

IV.   Display slide of doe.
    A. You can collect "trophies" you can enjoy forever.
    B. Display slide of buck.
    C. Not all hunters are killers: the film-hunter celebrates life, not death.

Scrambled Outline II

The following material is randomly presented. Arrange it in an outline format that follows the conventions of coordination and subordination. Be sure that each point relates directly to the point that precedes it.

1. There are existing organizations that students can support to help curb sexual assault rates.

2. Student crime watch patrols could help curb rates and theft and assault at night.

3. Per capita rates of sexual assault is higher on campus than in many of our larger cities.

4. Today we've discussed the growing problem of crime on campus, and what we, as students, can do about it.

5. Only you can lessen the chances that someday you or someone you love might become another victim.

6. As a victim of campus crime myself, I've become intimately concerned with this issue.

7. Only organized student involvement can help stem the tide of crime on campus.

8. We students should conduct a campaign against campus crime.

9. Last year seven cars and forty-two bicycles were stolen on campus.

10. "Take Back the Night" has been working to raise rape awareness and its effects on women for years.

11. The problem of campus crime has been growing steadily for years.

12. Can anyone imagine being robbed or even raped at gun-point in your own dorm building?

13. Student representatives could help pressure the administration to tighten campus security measures.

14. Rates of physical and violent assaults reported have increased 17% since 1990.

15. Today, I'm going to talk to you about the growing problem of crime on campus, and offer some solutions we can take to help stem the tide.

16. "Men Against Rape" needs volunteers to escort women on campus during evening hours.

17. Students could form a campus-wide "crime watch" program that works in cooperation with campus security.

18. To persuade my audience to conduct a campaign against campus crime.

Checklist for Using Presentation Aids

_____ Will my presentation aid enhance understanding?

_____ Is my presentation aid easy to understand?

_____ Is there enough information on my presentation aid?

_____ Is there too much information on my presentation aid?

_____ Is my presentation aid neat?

_____ Is the print on my presentation aid large enough for all audience members to read?

_____ Is everything on my presentation aid drawn to scale?

_____ Do I have the necessary equipment to use my presentation aid?

_____ Do I know how to use the equipment?

_____ Will I need tape or thumbtacks to position my presentation aid?

_____ Have I practiced presenting my speech using my presentation aid?

_____ Could I give my speech just as well, if not better, without my presentation aid?

Guide for Evaluating a Presentation

1. Name, title, and/or position of speaker:

2. Subject, date, and time of speech:

3. Occasion for speech, including sponsoring group:

4. Location and physical setting of speech:

5. Mode of presentation (impromptu, memorized, manuscript, extemporaneous):

6. Discussion of appropriateness and effectiveness of mode of presentation:

7. Description and discussion of speaker's voice:

8. Discussion of appropriateness and effectiveness of rate of speaking (including the use of pauses):

9. Discussion of appropriateness and effectiveness of loudness (including any problems with equipment such as microphone squeal):

10. Discussion of speaker's vocal variety:

11. Discussion of speaker's articulation, enunciation, pronunciation, or dialect:

12. Discussion of speaker's use of body language (including facial expressions, eye contact, movement, gestures, and appearance):

13. Suggestions you would give this speaker for improving presentation skills:

Guide for Evaluation of Voice and Articulation

Speaker's Name_____ Evaluated by _____

1. What did you feel was the most effective aspect of the speaker's voice and articulation?

_____

_____

2. What did you feel was the least effective aspect of the speaker's voice and articulation?

_____

_____

3. Should the speaker try to raise or lower his/her habitual pitch? _____

4. Does the speaker tend to speak too rapidly or too slowly? _____

5. Does the speaker use pauses effectively? _____

6. Does the speaker speak too quietly or too loudly? _____

7. Does the speaker have enough vocal variety? _____

8. Does the speaker have acceptable articulation and enunciation? _____

9. Are any words mispronounced? _____

10. Is the speaker's dialect acceptable? _____

11. What recommendations would you make for improvement? _____

_____

Guide for Evaluating Impromptu Presentations

Speaker _____ Topic _____ Date _____

5 = excellent   4 = good   3 = average   2 = below average   1 = poor

Opened with an introduction	5	4	3	2	1
Main ideas were previewed	5	4	3	2	1
Main ideas were easily identified	5	4	3	2	1
Main ideas were adapted to audience	5	4	3	2	1
Main ideas were properly supported	5	4	3	2	1
Main ideas were easy to follow	5	4	3	2	1
Main ideas were summarized	5	4	3	2	1
Concluding remarks reflected on meaning	5	4	3	2	1
Speaker maintained good eye contact	5	4	3	2	1
Gestures were used effectively	5	4	3	2	1
Rate of speaking was appropriate	5	4	3	2	1
Loudness level was appropriate	5	4	3	2	1
Vocal variety was appropriate	5	4	3	2	1

Comments:_____

_____

_____

_____

_____

Grade: _____

Evaluation Form for Question and Answer Sessions

Speaker _____ Topic _____ Date _____

5 = excellent   4 = good   3 = average   2 = below average   1 = poor   NA = not applicable

Actively encouraged questions	5	4	3	2	1	NA
Well-prepared to answer questions	5	4	3	2	1	NA
Repeated or paraphrased questions	5	4	3	2	1	NA
Maintained eye contact with audience	5	4	3	2	1	NA
Answers short and to the point	5	4	3	2	1	NA
Defused loaded questions	5	4	3	2	1	NA
Handled non-questions appropriately	5	4	3	2	1	NA
Maintained control	5	4	3	2	1	NA
Observed time limits	5	4	3	2	1	NA
Concluded by refocusing on main points of prepared message	5	4	3	2	1	NA

Comments:_____

_____

_____

_____

_____

Grade: _____

Evaluation Form for Televised Presentations

Student _____ Topic _____ Date _____

5 = excellent 4 = good 3 = average 2 = below average 1 = poor NA = not applicable

Speech appropriately timed	5	4	3	2	1	NA
Manuscript written in good oral style	5	4	3	2	1	NA
Colorful, memorable language	5	4	3	2	1	NA
Point, reason/example, restatement	5	4	3	2	1	NA
Sufficient previews and summaries	5	4	3	2	1	NA
Neat, well-groomed appearance	5	4	3	2	1	NA
Appropriate attire	5	4	3	2	1	NA
Good posture	5	4	3	2	1	NA
Conversational presentation	5	4	3	2	1	NA
Good use of vocal variety	5	4	3	2	1	NA
Eye contact through camera	5	4	3	2	1	NA
Gestures appropriately restrained	5	4	3	2	1	NA
Maintained demeanor through fade-out	5	4	3	2	1	NA

Comments:_____

_____

_____

_____

_____

Grade: _____

Using Language Effectively

Checklist for Language Usage

Complete the following checklist after you have prepared and practiced your speech. Ask a friend to listen to your speech and provide you with feedback on the checklist.

_____ Was my language clear and simple?

_____ Did I translate technical terms into lay language?

_____ Was I guilty of using jargon?

_____ Was my language colorful and vivid?

_____ Did I create memorable images for my audience?

_____ Was my language appropriately concrete?

_____ Did I use words correctly?

_____ Did I use strategic repetition?

_____ Did I avoid unnecessary repetition?

_____ Did I use any figures of speech?

_____ Was my language appropriate for the speaking situation?

_____ Did my language foster identification with the audience?

How Much Is?

some?   _____

a lot?   _____

a little?   _____

a whole lot?   _____

scads?   _____

a trifle?   _____

just a tad?   _____

many?   _____

a good many?   _____

several?   _____

not many?   _____

New Adages for Old

Where there's a will _____

Don't put all your eggs _____

Where there's smoke _____

Time and tide _____

Don't put the cart _____

A rolling stone _____

A bird in the hand _____

A stitch in time _____

He/she who hesitates _____

Look before you _____

Checklist for Preparing an Informative Speech

_____ I have selected a worthwhile topic.

_____ I have focused my topic so I can handle it in the time allotted to speak.

_____ I have done research to develop responsible knowledge on my topic.

_____ I have organized my material into an appropriate design.

_____ I have developed a working outline that I have revised as needed.

_____ I have prepared a formal outline that includes works cited.

_____ I have practiced presenting my speech using my formal outline for prompts.

_____ I have prepared a key word outline.

_____ I have practiced presenting my speech using my key word outline.

Topic Approval Form for an Informative Speech

Name: _____

Instructor: _____

Class Meeting Time: _____

Present two topic ideas for your informative speech. Write out the message you want the audience to get from your speech. Indicate which topic idea you would be most interested in developing.

Topic: _____

Message: _____

_____

_____

*   *   *   *   *   *   *   *

Topic: _____

Message: _____

_____

_____

What Design to Use When

Design	Use When
Spatial	Your topic can be discussed by how it is positioned in a physical setting or natural environment. It allows you to take your audience on an orderly "oral tour" of your topic as you move from place to place.
Sequential	Your topic can be arranged in a time sequence. It is useful for describing a process as a series of steps or explaining a subject as a series of historical landmark developments. Useful for presenting a plan of action in persuasive speeches.
Categorical	Your topic has natural or customary divisions. Each category becomes a main point for development. Useful when you need to organize large amounts of material. Useful in persuasive speeches to demonstrate that a plan will be <u>safe</u>, <u>inexpensive</u>, and <u>effective</u>, or to organize causes and consequences.
Comparative	Your topic is new to your audience, abstract, technical, or simply difficult to comprehend. Helps make material more meaningful by comparing or contrasting it with something the audience already knows and understands. Useful in persuasive speeches when you want to demonstrate why your proposal is superior to another. Especially good for speeches in which you contend with opposing views.
Causation	Your topic involves a situation, condition, or event that is best understood in terms of its underlying causes. May also be used to predict the future from existing conditions. Useful in persuasive speeches for discussing the causes and consequences of a problem.
Problem-solution	Your topic presents a problem that needs to be solved and a solution that will solve it. Good both for speeches involving attitudes and urging action.
Stock Issues	Your topic is one about which reasonable listeners might have questions they want answered before accepting your proposal.
Motivated Sequence	Your topic calls for action as the final phase of a five-step process that also involves, in order, arousing attention, demonstrating need, satisfying need, picturing the results, and calling for action.
Refutative	You must answer strong opposition on a topic before you can establish your position. The major opposing claims become main points for development. Attack weakest points first and avoid personal attacks.

Informative Speech Evaluation Form

Name _____ Date _____ Topic _____ Grade_____

General

_____ Did the speaker seem committed to the topic?
_____ Did the speech fulfill the specifics of the assignment?
_____ Was the speech adapted to fit the audience?
_____ Did the speech promote identification among topic, audience, and speaker?
_____ Was purpose of the speech clear?
_____ Was the topic handled with imagination and freshness?
_____ Did the speech meet high ethical standards?

Substance

_____ Was the topic worthwhile?
_____ Had the speaker done sufficient research?
_____ Were the main ideas supported with reliable information?
_____ Was testimony used appropriately?
_____ Were sources documented properly?
_____ Were examples and narratives used effectively?

Structure

_____ Did the introduction arouse interest?
_____ Did the introduction adequately preview the message?
_____ Was the speech easy to follow?
_____ Could you identify the main points of the speech?
_____ Were transitions used to tie the speech together?
_____ Did the conclusion help you remember the speech?

Presentation

_____ Was the language clear, simple, and direct?
_____ Was the language colorful?
_____ Were grammar and pronunciations correct?
_____ Was the speech presented extemporaneously?
_____ Were notes used unobtrusively?
_____ Was the speech presented enthusiastically?
_____ Did the speaker maintain good eye contact?
_____ Did the presentation sound "conversational"?
_____ Did gestures and body language complement ideas?
_____ Was the speaker's voice expressive?
_____ Were the rate and loudness appropriate to the material?
_____ Did the speaker use pauses appropriately?
_____ Did presentation aids make the message clearer or more memorable?
_____ Were presentation aids skillfully integrated into the speech?
_____ Was the presentation free from distracting mannerisms?

Comments:

Guidelines for Using a Spatial Design

You should use a spatial design when your subject involves places or objects that can be put in a physical arrangement. This design takes your listeners on a systematic and orderly tour of your subject or systematically describes an arrangement so that your audience may visualize it accurately.

To develop the body of a speech using a spatial design, select a starting point and a direction of movement for the verbal journey on which you will take your listeners. Move in an orderly manner. Start a route and stay with it. Try not to backtrack or jump from place to place. Your speech should build in interest as you move along to the last place which should be the most interesting.

Outline Worksheet: Spatial Design

TITLE (Optional)_____

Topic: _____

Specific Purpose: _____
_____

Thesis Statement: _____
_____

Introduction

Attention material: _____
_____

Credibility material: _____
_____

Preview: _____
_____

(Transition into body of speech)

_____

Body

I. Main point #1 (location 1) _____
_____

    A. (subpoint) _____

    _____

    B. (subpoint) _____

    _____

(Transition into main point 2)

_____

II. Main point #2 (location 2) _____
_____

A. (subpoint)_____

_____

B. (subpoint)_____

_____

(Transition into main point 3)

_____

III. Main point #3 (location 3) _____

_____

A. (subpoint)_____

_____

B. (subpoint)_____

_____

(Transition into main point 4)

_____

IV. Main point # 4: (location 4) _____

_____

A. (subpoint)_____

_____

B. (subpoint)_____

_____

(Transition into main point 5)

_____

_____

V. Main point # 5: (location 5) _____

_____

A. (subpoint)_____

_____

B. (subpoint)_____

_____

(Transition into conclusion)

_____

Conclusion

Summary : _____

_____

Concluding remarks: _____

_____

Works Consulted:

Checklist for a Spatial Design

_____ I have selected a topic that involves places or things that can be located physically.

_____ I have clearly stated the purpose of my speech.

_____ My thesis statement is written as a complete declarative sentence

_____ My introduction gains attention and interest, establishes my credibility, and previews the main points of my message.

_____ My first main point is the starting point for the verbal journey of my speech.

_____ My speech moves from place to place in an orderly fashion.

_____ My speech builds interest as it moves from location to location.

_____ I have adequate supporting material for each main point in my speech.

_____ I have positioned my subpoints under the main points to which they are related.

_____ My conclusion contains a summary that recaps my message and remarks that reflect on the meaning and significance of the speech.

_____ I have provided transitions where they are needed to make my speech flow smoothly.

_____ I have compiled a list of works consulted in the preparation of my speech.

Guidelines for Using a Sequential Design

A sequential design may be used to present the steps of a process or to provide an historical perspective on a subject.

When using a sequential design to present the steps in a process, you must first determine the necessary steps and the order in which they must take place. These steps become the main points of the speech. For an oral presentation you should not try to discuss more than five steps. If you have more than this, see if you can cluster some of them into subpoints. Be sure to enumerate the steps as you present them so that the audience can follow your message.

When using a sequential design to present an historical perspective on a subject, be sure to follow a systematic chronological sequence. Do not jump around in time (ie. start with 1990, jump back to 1942, fast forward to 1971) or the speech will be hard for your listeners to follow. You can either begin with the beginnings of a subject and trace it to a later point in time or begin with the present and trace the subject back to its origins. When presenting a historical perspective, it is important to narrow your topic to manageable proportions by selecting the most important historical occurrences. Your speech should telescope time.

Outline Worksheet: Sequential Design

TITLE (Optional)_____

Topic: _____

Specific Purpose: _____

_____

Thesis Statement: _____

_____

Introduction

Attention material: _____

_____

Credibility material: _____

_____

Preview: _____

_____

(Transition into body of speech)

_____

Body

I. Main point #1 (step or occurrence 1) _____

_____

    A. (subpoint) _____

    _____

    B. (subpoint) _____

    _____

(Transition into main point 2)

_____

II. Main point #2 (step or occurrence 2) _____

_____

    A. (subpoint)_____

    _____

    B. (subpoint)_____

    _____

(Transition into main point 3)

_____

III. Main point #3 (step or occurrence 3) _____

_____

    A. (subpoint)_____

    _____

    B. (subpoint)_____

    _____

(Transition into main point 4)

_____

IV. Main point # 4: (step or occurrence 4) _____

_____

    A. (subpoint)_____

    _____

    B. (subpoint)_____

    _____

(Transition into main point 5)

_____

IV. Main point # 5: (step or occurrence 5) _____

_____

A. (subpoint)_____

_____

B. (subpoint)_____

_____

(Transition into conclusion)

_____

Conclusion

Summary: _____

_____

Concluding remarks: _____

_____

Works Consulted:

Checklist for a Sequential Design

_____ My topic involves a process that can be explained as a series of steps or a subject on which I wish to provide a historical perspective.

_____ I have clearly stated the purpose of my speech.

_____ My thesis statement is written as a complete declarative sentence

_____ My introduction gains attention and interest, establishes my credibility, and previews the main points of my message.

_____ I have determined the main steps that must be taken (if applicable).

_____ I have arranged the steps in the order in which they must be taken (if applicable).

_____ I have selected the major occurrences or developments related to my topic (if applicable).

_____ I have presented the occurrences chronologically (if applicable).

_____ I have adequate supporting material for each main point in my speech.

_____ I have positioned my subpoints under the main points to which they are related.

_____ My conclusion contains a summary that recaps my message and remarks that reflect on the meaning and significance of the speech.

_____ I have provided transitions where they are needed to make my speech flow smoothly.

_____ I have compiled a list of works consulted in the preparation of my speech.

Guidelines for Using a Categorical Design

You should use a categorical design for subjects that have natural or customary divisions. This design allows you to organize large amounts of material into a manageable format. Do not use a categorical design by default--because you are too lazy to think of any other way to arrange your information.

When using a categorical design each category becomes a main point for the development of your speech. Limit yourself to five or fewer main points in a short speech. You should begin and end with the most important categories since the first and last areas covered are the most easily remembered.

Outline Worksheet: Categorical Design

TITLE (Optional)_____

Topic:_____

Specific Purpose: _____

_____

Thesis Statement: _____

_____

Introduction

Attention material: _____

_____

Credibility material: _____

_____

Preview: _____

_____

(Transition into body of speech)

_____

Body

I. Main point #1 (first category) _____

_____

    A. (subpoint) _____

_____

    B. (subpoint) _____

_____

(Transition into main point 2)

_____

II. Main point #2 (second category) _____

_____

    A. (subpoint)_____

        _____

    B. (subpoint) _____

        _____

(Transition into main point 3)

_____

III. Main point #3 (third category) _____

_____

    A. (subpoint)_____

        _____

    B. (subpoint)_____

        _____

(Transition into main point 4)

_____

IV. Main point # 4: (fourth category) _____

_____

    A. (subpoint)_____

        _____

    B. (subpoint)_____

        _____

(Transition into main point 5)

_____

V. Main point # 5: (fifth category) _____

_____

    A. (subpoint)_____

      _____

    B. (subpoint)_____

      _____

(Transition into conclusion)

_____

Conclusion

Summary: _____

_____

Concluding remarks: _____

_____

Works Consulted:

Checklist for a Categorical Design

_____ I have selected a topic that has natural or customary divisions.

_____ I have clearly stated the purpose of my speech.

_____ My thesis statement is written as a complete declarative sentence

_____ My introduction gains attention and interest, establishes my credibility, and previews the main points of my message.

_____ I have no more than five categories as main points in my speech.

_____ I have arranged my speech so that the most important categories are presented first and last.

_____ I have positioned my subpoints under the main points to which they are related.

_____ My conclusion contains a summary that recaps my message and remarks that reflect on the meaning and significance of the speech.

_____ I have provided transitions where they are needed to make my speech flow smoothly.

_____ I have compiled a list of works consulted in the preparation of my speech.

Guidelines for Using a Comparative Design

You may wish to use a comparative design if your topic is new to your audience, abstract, highly technical, or simply difficult to understand. The comparative design aids understanding by relating your topic to something the audience already knows and comprehends. It may take the form of a literal analogy, a figurative analogy, or a comparison and contrast showing both similarities and differences.

The body of a speech using a comparative design may include up to five main similarities or differences. In a literal analogy, the topics are drawn from the same area: for example, word processing and typing are two forms of producing written information using a keyboard so the comparison between them is literal. In a figurative analogy, the speaker draws together topics from different areas: for example, relating the body's struggle against infection to a military campaign by identifying who or what makes up the armies, how they fight, and the consequences of victory or defeat. In a comparison and contrast design you show how two things are both similar and different.

Outline Worksheet: Comparative Design

TITLE (Optional)_____

Topic: _____

Specific Purpose: _____

_____

Thesis Statement: _____

_____

Introduction

Attention material: _____

_____

Credibility material: _____

_____

Preview: _____

_____

(Transition into body of speech)

_____

Body

I. Main point #1 (first similarity or difference) _____

_____

    A. (subpoint) _____

_____

    B. (subpoint) _____

_____

(Transition into main point 2)

_____

II. Main point #2 (second similarity or difference) _____

_____

    A. (subpoint)_____

        _____

    B. (subpoint)_____

        _____

(Transition into main point 3)

_____

III. Main point #3 (third similarity or difference) _____

_____

    A. (subpoint)_____

        _____

    B. (subpoint)_____

        _____

(Transition into main point 4)

_____

IV. Main point # 4: (fourth similarity or difference) _____

_____

    A. (subpoint)_____

        _____

    B. (subpoint)_____

        _____

(Transition into main point 5)

_____

V. Main point # 5: (fifth similarity or difference) _____

_____

    A. (subpoint)_____

_____

    B. (subpoint) _____

_____

(Transition into conclusion)

_____

Conclusion

Summary: _____

_____

Concluding remarks: _____

_____

Works Consulted:

Checklist for a Comparative Design

_____ I have selected a topic that is unfamiliar, abstract, or otherwise difficult to understand.

_____ The purpose of my speech is to compare and/or contrast two or more similar or dissimilar objects, ideas, situations, people, or events.

_____ I have clearly stated the purpose of my speech.

_____ My thesis statement is written as a complete declarative sentence.

_____ My introduction gains attention and interest, establishes my credibility, and previews the main points of my message.

_____ Each of my main points addresses one point of comparison or contrast.

_____ Each of my main points is supported with facts, statistics, testimony, examples, or narratives.

_____ The comparison or contrasts I make are not strained.

_____ I have positioned subpoints under the main points to which they are related.

_____ I have included a summary statement that reviews the comparisons and contrasts.

_____ I have prepared concluding remarks that reflect on the meaning and significance of my message.

_____ I have provided transitions where they are needed to make my speech flow smoothly.

_____ I have compiled a list of works consulted in the preparation of my speech.

Topic Approval Form for a Persuasive Speech

Name: _____

Instructor: _____

Class Meeting Time: _____

Present two topic ideas for your persuasive speech. Write out the message you want the audience to get from your speech. Indicate which topic idea you would be most interested in developing.

Topic: _____

Message: _____

_____

_____

* * * * * * * *

Topic: _____

Message: _____

_____

_____

Persuasive Speech Evaluation Form

Name _____ Date _____ Topic _____ Grade_____

General
_____ Did the speaker seem committed to the topic?
_____ Did the speech fulfill the specifics of the assignment?
_____ Was the speech adapted to fit the audience?
_____ Did the speech promote identification among topic, audience, and speaker?
_____ Was purpose of the speech clear?
_____ Was the topic handled with imagination and freshness?
_____ Did the speech meet high ethical standards?

Substance
_____ Was the topic worthwhile?
_____ Had the speaker done sufficient research?
_____ Were the main ideas supported with reliable information?
_____ Was testimony used appropriately?
_____ Were sources documented properly?
_____ Were examples and narratives used effectively?
_____ Were appropriate proofs used?
_____ Was the reasoning clear?
_____ Did the reasoning follow an acceptable logical pattern?

Structure
_____ Did the introduction arouse interest?
_____ Did the introduction adequately preview the message?
_____ Was the speech easy to follow?
_____ Could you identify the main points of the speech?
_____ Were transitions used to tie the speech together?
_____ Did the conclusion help you remember the speech?

Presentation
_____ Was the language clear, simple, and direct?
_____ Was the language colorful?
_____ Were grammar and pronunciations correct?
_____ Was the speech presented extemporaneously?
_____ Were notes used unobtrusively?
_____ Was the speech presented enthusiastically?
_____ Did the speaker maintain good eye contact?
_____ Did the presentation sound "conversational"?
_____ Did gestures and body language complement ideas?
_____ Was the speaker's voice expressive?
_____ Were the rate and loudness appropriate to the material?
_____ Did the speaker use pauses appropriately?
_____ Did presentation aids make the message clearer or more memorable?
_____ Were presentation aids skillfully integrated into the speech?
_____ Was the presentation free from distracting mannerisms?

Comments:

Guidelines for Using a Causation Design

You may wish to use a causation design for a speech of explanation that tries to make the world and the things in it more understandable. The causation design explains a situation, condition, or event in terms of the causes that led up to it.

The body of a causation design typically begins with a description of existing conditions, then probes for its causes. The description of existing conditions becomes the first main point in the speech with the causes being subsequent main points.

The causes may be separated into categories which can then be arranged in order of their importance. The causes may also be presented in an historical design which may begin with the distant past and work up to the present, begin with the present and work back to the origin of the situation, or begin with the present and make projections into the future.

Outline Worksheet: Causation Design

TITLE (Optional)_____

Topic: _____

Specific Purpose: _____

_____

Thesis Statement: _____

_____

Introduction

Attention material: _____

_____

Credibility material: _____

_____

Preview: _____

_____

(Transition into body of speech)

_____

Body

I. Main point #1 (description of existing conditions) _____

_____

    A. (subpoint) _____

_____

    B. (subpoint) _____

_____

(Transition into main point 2)

_____

II. Main point #2 (first cause) _____

_____

A. (subpoint)_____

_____

B. (subpoint) _____

_____

(Transition into main point 3)

_____

III. Main point #3 (second cause) _____

_____

A. (subpoint)_____

_____

B. (subpoint)_____

_____

(Transition into main point 4)

_____

IV. Main point # 4: (third cause) _____

_____

A. (subpoint) _____

_____

B. (subpoint)_____

_____

(Transition into main point 5)

_____

V. Main point # 5: (fourth cause) _____

_____

A. (subpoint)_____

_____

B. (subpoint)_____

_____

(Transition into conclusion)

_____

Conclusion

Summary: _____

_____

Concluding remarks: _____

_____

Works Consulted:

Checklist for a Causation Design

_____ I have selected a topic that involves a situation, condition, or event that can best be understood in terms of its causes.

_____ I have clearly stated the purpose of my speech.

_____ My thesis statement is written as a complete declarative sentence.

_____ My introduction gains attention and interest, establishes my credibility, and previews the main points of my message.

_____ The first main point of my speech describes the present condition, situation, or event.

_____ Subsequent main points of my speech explain the causes of the condition, situation, or event.

_____ The main points containing causes are arranged either categorically in terms of their importance or chronologically (see categorical and sequential designs).

_____ I have been careful not to oversimplify the cause-effect relationships.

_____ I have positioned my subpoints under the main points to which they are related.

_____ My conclusion contains a summary that recaps my message and remarks that reflect on the meaning and significance of the speech.

_____ I have provided transitions where they are needed to make my speech flow smoothly.

_____ I have compiled a list of works consulted in the preparation of my speech.

Guidelines for Using a Problem-Solution Design

You may wish to use a problem-solution design when you must convince your audience they should face up to a specific problem and that you have a solution that will deal with it. It is sometimes difficult to convince people that there really is a problem that deserves or even demands their attention. People often ignore problems until they reach a critical stage when drastic action is necessary. You can counteract this by depicting the crisis that will arise unless the audience makes the changes you suggest. The solution phase of a problem-solution design typically involves changing an attitude or taking action.

The body of a problem-solution design usually has only two main points: the presentation of the problem and the presentation of the solution. Subpoints under the problem main point describe the problem, highlight its importance, and suggest what might happen if the problem is ignored. Subpoints under the solution main point describe the solution, show how it solves the problem, present a plan of action, and picture the results of its implementation.

Outline Worksheet: Problem-Solution Design

TITLE (Optional)_____

Topic: _____

Specific Purpose: _____

_____

Thesis Statement: _____

_____

Introduction

Attention material: _____

_____

Credibility material: _____

_____

Preview: _____

_____

(Transition into body of speech)

_____

Body

I. Main point #1 (Statement of problem) _____

_____

    A. (Description of problem) _____

_____

        1. (Signs, symptoms, effects of problem) _____

_____

        2. (Example, narrative, or testimony) _____

_____

B. (Importance of problem) _____

_____

    1. (Extent of problem)_____

_____

        a. (Facts/statistics) _____

_____

        b. (Expert testimony) _____

_____

    2. (Who is affected) _____

_____

        a. (Facts/statistics) _____

_____

        b. (Example/narrative) _____

_____

C. (Consequences of problem) _____

_____

    1. (Expert testimony)_____

_____

    2. (Example/narrative) _____

_____

(Transition into main point 2)

_____

II. Main point #2 (Statement of solution) _____

_____

A. (Description of solution)_____

_____

    1. (How solution fits problem) _____

_____

     a. (More than symptom relief) _____

_____

     b. (Is workable) _____

_____

2. (How solution can be implemented) _____

_____

     a. (Plan of action) _____

_____

         (1) (Step 1 of plan) _____

_____

         (2) (Step 2 of plan) _____

_____

         (3) (Step 3 of plan) _____

_____

         (4) (Step 4 of plan) _____

_____

     b. (Costs and efforts) _____

_____

B. (Picture results) _____

_____

1. (Describe expected results) _____

_____

2. (When results expected) _____

_____

3. (Additional benefits) _____

_____

(Transition into conclusion)

_____

Conclusion

Summary: _____

_____

Concluding remarks:_____

_____

Works Consulted:

Checklist for a Problem-Solution Design

_____ I have selected a topic that involves a problem that needs to be solved.

_____ I have clearly stated the purpose of my speech.

_____ My thesis statement is written as a complete declarative sentence.

_____ My introduction gains attention and interest, establishes my credibility, and previews the main points of my message.

_____ My first main point presents the problem.

_____ My subpoints for the first main point describe the problem, show its importance, and demonstrate the consequences of inaction.

_____ I have adequate supporting material for each of my subppoints relating to the problem.

_____ My second main points presents my solution to the problem.

_____ My subpoints for the second main point demonstrate how the solution addresses the problem, describe a plan of action, and picture the results of the solution.

_____ I have adequate supporting material for each of my subppoints relating to the solution.

_____ My conclusion contains a summary that recaps my message and remarks that reflect on the meaning and significance of my speech.

_____ I have provided transitions where they are needed to make my speech flow smoothly.

_____ I have compiled a list of works consulted in the preparation of my speech.

Guidelines for Using a Motivated Sequence Design

You may wish to use a motivated sequence design for a persuasive speech intended to move people to action. The motivated sequence design is a highly structured variation of the problem solution design. It concentrates on awakening an awareness of a need and then shows how that need can be satisfied concluding with an explicit call for action. The motivated sequence contains five steps: 1) focusing attention on a problem, 2) demonstrating a need, 3) presenting a solution to satisfy that need, 4) visualizing the results of the implementation of the solution, and 5) issuing a call to action.

The first step in the motivated sequence design comes in the introduction of the speech. In the motivated sequence design the introduction should arouse attention and directly focus this attention on the problem that will be addressed in the speech.

The second through fourth steps in the motivated sequence design are covered in the body of the speech which will typically contain three main points. The first main point of the body of the speech covers step 2 of the motivated sequence design. It would be used to demonstrate a need related to the problem. The second main point of the body of the speech covers step 3 of the motivated sequence design. It should present a detailed plan of action to satisfy the need. The third main point of the body of the speech covers step 4 of the motivated sequence design. It should picture the positive results that will occur if the plan is adopted and/or the negative results that might be expected if the plan is ignored.

The fifth step in the motivated sequence design comes in the conclusion of the speech. It is a call for action.

When using the motivated sequence design, audience analysis is extremely important. For example, if the audience already recognizes that there is a need for action, that step in the sequence can be covered briefly and the major thrust of the speech would address the plan, visualization of results, and the call for action. Similarly, if the audience is convinced of the need and familiar with the plan, but needs its momentum renewed or needs to be prodded into action, the focus of the speech would be on visualizing the results and calling for action.

Outline Worksheet: Motivated Sequence Design

TITLE (Optional)_____

Topic: _____

Specific Purpose: _____

_____

Thesis Statement: _____

_____

Introduction

Attention material (focus attention on problem): _____

_____

Credibility material: _____

_____

Preview: _____

_____

(Transition into body of speech)

_____

Body

I. Main point 1 (Statement of need for action) _____

_____

    A. (Description of problem) _____

_____

        1. (Signs, symptoms, effects of problem)_____

_____

        2. (Example, narrative, or testimony)_____

_____

B. (Importance of problem) _____

_____

    1. (Extent of problem) _____

_____

        a. (Facts/statistics) _____

_____

        b. (Expert testimony) _____

_____

    2. (Who is affected) _____

_____

        a. (Facts/statistics) _____

_____

        b. (Example/narrative)_____

_____

(Transition into main point 2)

_____

II. Main point #2 (Present solution that satisfies need) _____

_____

A. (Description of solution)_____

_____

    1. (How solution satisfies need) _____

_____

    2. (How solution can be implemented) _____

_____

        a. (Plan of action)_____

_____

          (1) (Step 1 of plan) _____

_____

(2) (Step 2 of plan) _____

_____

(3) (Step 3 of plan) _____

_____

(4) (Step 4 of plan) _____

_____

(Transition into main point 3)

_____

III. (Visualize results)_____

_____

    1. (Describe expected results of action) _____

_____

    2. (Describe consequences of inaction)_____

_____

(Transition into conclusion)

_____

Conclusion

Summary: _____

_____

Call for action:_____

_____

Works Consulted:

Checklist for a Motivated Sequence Design

_____ I have selected a topic that involves a problem that needs to be solved with action.

_____ I have clearly stated the purpose of my speech.

_____ My thesis statement is written as a complete declarative sentence.

_____ My introduction focuses attention on the problem, establishes my credibility, and previews my message.

_____ The first main point in my speech establishes the need for action.

_____ The second main point in my speech details a plan of action that satisfies the need.

_____ The third main point in my speech visualizes the results of action and the consequences of inaction.

_____ I have appropriate supporting material for each main point in my speech.

_____ The conclusion of my speech contains a summary statement and ends with a call for action.

_____ I have provided transitions where they are needed to make my speech flow smoothly.

_____ I have compiled a list of works consulted in the preparation of my speech.

Guidelines for Using a Refutative Design

You may wish to use a refutative design to raise doubts about, damage, or even destroy an opposing position by pointing out its weaknesses and inconsistencies. To make an effective refutation, you must be thoroughly familiar with the points the opposition would make in an argument. It is wise to attack the weakest points or arguments first. Don't try to refute more than three points or arguments in a short classroom presentation. Base your refutations on faulty reasoning or inadequate evidence. Avoid personal attacks on opponents unless credibility issues are inescapable. If time permits, support an alternative point or argument to replace the one(s) you have refuted.

In the body of your speech your main points will be the points or arguments you are refuting or supporting. Refutation follows a five step sequence: 1) state the point you will refute and explain its importance to the opposing position, 2) tell how you will refute the point, 3) present evidence to refute the point, 4) show how the evidence refutes the point, and 5) explain the significance of the refutation. A refutative speech is strengthened if you can support an alternative point or argument for each one that you refute. Use the same five steps to demonstrate the superiority of your position. The inclusion of a supported point helps to counteract the negativity associated with straight refutation and provides the audience with a sense of completeness and closure.

Outline Worksheet: Refutative Design

TITLE (Optional)_____

Topic: _____

Specific Purpose: _____

_____

Thesis Statement: _____

_____

Introduction

Attention material: _____

_____

Credibility material: _____

_____

Preview: _____

_____

(Transition into body of speech)

_____

Body

I. Main point #1(first point you will refute/weakest point of opposition) _____

_____

    A. (Explain importance of point) _____

_____

    B. (Explain how you will refute point) _____

_____

    C. (Present evidence to refute point) _____

_____

    1. (Facts/figures) _____

    _____

    2. (Expert testimony) _____

    _____

  D. (Explain how evidence refutes point) _____

  _____

  E. (Explain significance of refutation) _____

  _____

    1. (Facts/figures/expert testimony) _____

    _____

    2. (Example/narrative) _____

    _____

(Transition into main point 2)

_____

II. Main point #2 (second point you will refute or counterpoint you will support) _____

_____

  A. (Explain importance of point) _____

  _____

  B. (Explain how you will refute/support point) _____

  _____

  C. (Present evidence to refute/support point) _____

  _____

1. (Facts/figures) _____

_____

2. (Expert testimony) _____

_____

D. (Explain how evidence refutes/supports point) _____

_____

E. (Explain significance of refutation/support) _____

_____

1. (Facts/figures/expert testimony) _____

_____

2. (Example/narrative) _____

_____

(Transition into main point 3)

_____

_____

III. Main point #3 (second/third point you will refute) _____

_____

A. (Explain importance of point) _____

_____

B. (Explain how you will refute point) _____

_____

C. (Present evidence to refute point) _____

_____

1. (Facts/figures) _____

_____

    2. (Expert testimony) _____

_____

D. (Explain how evidence refutes point) _____

_____

E. (Explain significance of refutation) _____

_____

    1. (Facts/figures/expert testimony) _____

_____

    2. (Example/narrative) _____

_____

(Transition into main point 4)

_____

IV. Main point #4 (next point you will refute or counterpoint you will support) _____

_____

A. (Explain importance of point) _____

_____

B. (Explain how you will refute/support point) _____

_____

C. (Present evidence to refute/support point) _____

_____

    1. (Facts/figures) _____

_____

2. (Expert testimony) _____

_____

D. (Explain how evidence refutes/supports point) _____

_____

E. (Explain significance of refutation/support) _____

_____

1. (Facts/figures/expert testimony) _____

_____

2. (Example/narrative) _____

_____

(Transition into conclusion)

_____

Conclusion

Summary: _____

_____

Concluding remarks: _____

_____

Works Consulted:

Checklist for a Refutative Design

_____ I have selected a topic that involves an issue that has strong opposition.

_____ I have clearly stated the purpose of my speech.

_____ My thesis statement is written as a complete declarative sentence.

_____ My introduction gains attention and interest, establishes my credibility, and previews the main points of my message.

_____ My first main point refutes the opposition's weakest point.

_____ Each main point for refutation is clearly stated and its importance explained.

_____ I describe how I will attack each point and present credible evidence to support my refutation.

_____ I clearly explain what each refutation means.

_____ I have supported a counterpoint for each point I have refuted following the same format used for each refutation.

_____ I have avoided personal attacks in my refutations.

_____ My conclusion contains a summary that recaps my message and concluding remarks that reflect on the meaning and significance of my speech.

_____ I have provided transitions where they are needed to make my speech flow smoothly.

_____ I have compiled a list of works consulted in preparation for my speech.

Find the Fallacy

1. In 1931, approximately 6,000 workers were killed in industrial accidents in the United States. In 1945, over 9,000 workers were killed in industrial accidents. The rate of workers killed in industrial accidents rose dramatically between 1931 and 1945.

2. If we allow the communists a toehold in San Salvador, Mexico will be next.

3. Because the Great Depression began during Hoover's presidency, it is safe to assume that his economic policies were its primary cause.

4. Don't listen to environmentalists complain about acid rain. They're just a bunch of pot-smoking hippies.

5. My brother got a bad grade in algebra. My roommate got a bad grade in algebra. The girl sitting next to me in history class got a bad grade in algebra. Nobody makes a good grade in that class!

6. You know she can't be a good Republican. Her father was a liberal.

7. What's good for General Motors is good for America.

8. Salaries are really good at Gulf State Bank. They average more than $62,000 per year.

9. Don't tell me about recycling and the environment. By not being a vegetarian, you are ultimately contributing to environmental destruction yourself.

10. Everyone knows that taxes are bad for the economy.

Topic Approval Form for a Ceremonial Speech

Name: _____

Instructor: _____

Class Meeting Time: _____

Present two topic ideas for your ceremonial speech. Write out the message you want the audience to get from your speech. Indicate which topic idea you would be most interested in developing.

Topic: _____

Message: _____

_____

_____

* * * * * * * *

Topic: _____

Message: _____

_____

_____

Ceremonial Speech Evaluation Form

Name _____ **Date** _____ **Topic** _____ **Grade** _____

General

_____ Did the speaker seem committed to the topic?
_____ Did the speech fulfill the specifics of the assignment?
_____ Did the speech promote identification among topic, audience, and speaker?
_____ Was purpose of the speech clear?
_____ Was the topic handled with imagination and freshness?

Substance and Structure

_____ Did the introduction arouse interest?
_____ Was the speech easy to follow?
_____ Could you identify the main points of the speech?
_____ Were the proper factors magnified in the presentation?
_____ Were main ideas supported by examples or narratives?
_____ Did the conclusion help you remember the speech?

Presentation

_____ Was the language clear and direct?
_____ Was the language appropriate to the occasion?
_____ Were grammar and pronunciations correct?
_____ Was the speech presented extemporaneously?
_____ Were notes used unobtrusively?
_____ Did the speaker maintain good eye contact?
_____ Did the presentation sound "conversational"?
_____ Did gestures and body language complement ideas?
_____ Was the speaker's voice expressive?
_____ Were the rate and loudness appropriate to the material?
_____ Did the speaker use pauses appropriately?
_____ Was the presentation free from distracting mannerisms?

Comments:

Checklist for Developing a Narrative Design

_____ I have described the setting in which my story will play out.

_____ I have established the context in which my story occurs.

_____ I have aroused audience interest by foreshadowing the characters in my story.

_____ I have aroused curiosity by foreshadowing the meaning of my story.

_____ I have selected a scene (or scenes) in which the action of my story will unfold.

_____ I have used colorful detail, picturesque language, and lively dialogue to bring the action to life.

_____ I have developed characters who are interesting because of their roles in the action.

_____ I have built suspense to bring my story to a climax.

_____ I reflect on the meaning of my story so that listeners get the point.

_____ My story leaves listeners with the feeling that they have met an interesting character(s) they will want to remember.

_____ My story teaches an important lesson that listeners can apply.

_____ I have used language skills to help listeners remember the message.

Outline Format for Narrative Design

Prologue

A. Setting and context of story: _____

_____

B. Foreshadowing characters: _____

_____

C. Foreshadowing meaning: _____

_____

Plot

A. Scene 1: _____

_____

B. Scene 2: _____

_____

C. Scene 3: _____

_____

Epilogue

A. Final scene: _____

_____

B. Lessons of the story: _____

_____

Works and People Consulted

Possible Topics for Narratives

The most exciting day of my life.

The worst day of my life.

How I met the person I am dating/married to.

A story my mother/father told me.

A story I want to tell my children.

A story that reflects my cultural background.

The scariest dream I ever had.

The wildest dream I ever had.

The sweetest dream I ever had.

How I learned how to laugh at myself.

How I learned the importance of telling the truth.

How I bought my first _____.

How I got taken for a sucker.

The story of my bravest hour.

How I decided on my major.

The funniest thing my pet ever did.

The funniest thing a family member of mine ever did.

The funniest thing I ever did.

The dumbest thing I ever did.

The smartest thing I ever did.

How I overcame a problem with _____.

The nicest thing anyone ever did for me.

The meanest thing anyone ever did to me.

HUMOR ORIENTATION SCALE*

Please respond to the following statements in terms of how well they describe your typical behavior. Use the following scale of agreement.

> 5 = Strongly Agree
> 4 = Agree
> 3 = Neutral
> 2 = Disagree
> 1 = Strongly Disagree

_____ 1. I regularly tell jokes or funny stories when I am with a group.

_____ 2. People usually laugh when I tell a joke or story.

_____ 3. I have no memory for jokes or funny stories.

_____ 4. I can be funny without having to rehearse a joke.

_____ 5. Being funny is a natural communication style with me.

_____ 6. I cannot tell a joke well.

_____ 7. People seldom ask me to tell stories.

_____ 8. My friends would say that I am a funny person.

_____ 9. People don't seem to pay close attention when I tell a joke.

_____ 10. Even funny jokes seem flat when I tell them.

_____ 11. I can easily remember jokes and stories.

_____ 12. People often ask me to tell jokes and stories.

_____ 13. My friends would not say that I am a funny person.

_____ 14. I don't tell jokes or stories even when asked to.

_____ 15. I tell stories and jokes very well.

_____ 16. Of all the people I know, I'm one of the funniest.

_____ 17. I use humor to communicate in a variety of situations.

* Adapted from Steve Booth-Butterfield and Melanie Booth-Butterfield, "Individual Differences in the Communication of Humorous Messages," SSCJ, Spring 1991, 32-40.

GROUP DISCUSSION PARTICIPANT EVALUATION FORM

Person being evaluated _____

Your name _____ Date _____

Use the following scale to describe the person assigned to you. Indicate your evaluation by circling one of the numbers to the left of each statement. You <u>must</u> describe and evaluate this student's performance.

1 = poor, 2 = below average, 3 = average, 4 = above average, 5 = superior

1 2 3 4 5   Appeared committed to the goals of the group

1 2 3 4 5   Participated frequently in group deliberations.

1 2 3 4 5   Contributions were clear, relevant, and helpful.

1 2 3 4 5   Performed task leadership functions.

1 2 3 4 5   Performed social leadership functions.

1 2 3 4 5   Helped resolve conflict within the group.

1 2 3 4 5   Encouraged participation of other group members.

1 2 3 4 5   Helped keep the discussion focused on the problem.

1 2 3 4 5   Contribution in comparison with other group members.

1 2 3 4 5   Emerged as the leader of this group.

Leadership Potential Questionnaire

Leadership is composed of many facets. The ability to establish confidence, respect, and good rapport is required. Many people are afraid of assuming a leadership role. Others grow into it although they feel at first they are not qualified. What about you?

This quiz is designed to help you measure your leadership potential by thinking back on real situations in your life and projecting yourself into possible future circumstances where leadership might be required. Its purpose is to start you <u>thinking about</u> your leadership potential. It is not a scientifically developed measuring instrument. Respond as honestly as you can to the following items and see what you can learn about your leadership potential.

1. Your instructions were not followed and everything got messed up. Why?
    A. You did not foresee all the blunders your subordinates could make.
    B. It seems impossible to get halfway intelligent people to work these days.
    C. You did not explain the assignment in sufficient detail.

2. You are asked to organize a group to improve your neighborhood. How would you react?
    A. Use an excuse, such as being too busy, to get out of it.
    B. Ask someone who had organized such a group before to help you.
    C. Feel flattered and accept the assignment, even though its a first for you.

3. Someone higher up in your group gives you an order. What are you most likely to do?
    A. Question the order and possibly suggest an alternative.
    B. Discuss the pros and cons and finally agree.
    C. An order is an order and I carry it through as best I can.

4. You read about the chaotic state of affairs in another country. Finally a strong person takes over and puts everything in better working order. How do you react to this news?
    A. Is he/she a dictator? I don't know and if so, so what?
    B. It was necessary to introduce strong measures. The people always have to be led; later on they can participate again in decisions.
    C. Had the people been properly informed, they would have taken the right measures themselves.

5. You read the following statement: "He was relentless. He drove himself and others. He did not rest until he had reached a goal." What is your reaction?
    A. I am just like him.
    B. He is an unhappy person. I prefer to enjoy myself.
    C. If he could relax in between it's okay, otherwise I pity him.

6. You read in a person's obituary that he never complimented anyone in his organization. He watched every little detail. Managers were fired at the slightest pretext. He was feared by everybody, but he created a successful company.
    A. That is a very heavy price to pay. Probably nobody really liked him.
    B. Sometimes that is the only way to lead. The end result is really the important thing.
    C. He might have been more successful had he been more human and caring.

Adapted from Ernest Dichter, <u>Total Self-Knowledge</u> (New York: Stein & Day, 1976), pp. 211-214. Copyright @1976 by Ernest Dichter. Originally published by Stein & Day, Inc. Reprinted with permission of Scarborough House/Publishers and the author.

What Kind of Leader are You?*

For each of the following questions, circle the answer that best applies to you.

Yes No   1. Do you enjoy "running the show"?

Yes No   2. Generally, do you think it's worth the time and effort to explain the reasons for a decision or policy before putting it into effect?

Yes No   3. Do you prefer the administrative end of your leadership job--planning, paperwork, and so on--to supervising or working directly with your subordinates?

Yes No   4. A stranger comes into your department and you know he's the new employee hired by one of your assistants. On approaching him, would you first ask <u>his</u> name rather than introducing yourself?

Yes No   5. Do you keep your people up-to-date as a matter of course on developments affecting the group?

Yes No   6. Do you find that in giving out assignments you tend to state the goals and leave the methods to your subordinates?

Yes No   7. Do you think that it's good common sense for a leader to keep aloof from his or her people because in the long run familiarity breeds lessened respect?

Yes No   8. It comes time to decide about a group outing. You've heard that the majority prefer to have it on Wednesday, but you're pretty sure Thursday would be better for all concerned. Would you put the question to a vote rather than make the decision yourself?

Yes No   9. If you had your way, would you make running your group a push-button affair with personal contacts and communications held to a minimum?

Yes No   10. Do you find it fairly easy to fire someone?

Yes No   11. Do you feel that the friendlier you are with your people, the better you'll be able to lead them?

Yes No   12. After considerable time, you figure out the answer to a work problem. You pass along the solution to an assistant who pokes it full of holes. Will you be annoyed that the problem is still unresolved rather than become angry with the assistant?

Yes No   13. Do you agree that one of the best ways to avoid problems of discipline is to provide adequate punishments for violations of rules?

Yes No   14. Your way of handling a situation is being criticized. Would you try to sell your viewpoint to your group rather than make it clear that, as boss, your decisions are final?

Yes No   15. Do you generally leave it up to your subordinates to contact you as far as informal, day-to-day communications are concerned?

Yes No   16. Do you feel that everyone in your group should have a certain amount of personal loyalty to you?

Yes No   17. Do you favor the practice of appointing committees to settle a problem rather than stepping in to decide on it yourself?

Yes No   18. Some experts say differences of opinion within a work group are healthy. Others feel that such differences indicate basic flaws in group unity. Do you agree with the first view?

Scoring and Interpretation

To get your score, circle the question numbers 1 through 18 to which you answered yes. Then compare your answers with the groupings below.

A.	1, 4, 7, 10, 13, 16.
B.	2, 5, 8, 11, 14, 17.
C.	3, 6, 9, 12, 15, 18.

If most of your yes answers correspond with Group A, chances are you tend to be an autocratic leader. If you total yes answers were highest in Group B, you probably have a predisposition toward being a participative leader. If Group C is the one in which you had the greatest number of yes answers, you are probably inclined toward being a free-rein leader.

* Adapted from <u>Mastery of Management</u> by Auren Uris by permission of the Berkeley Publishing Company, (1968).

What Kind of Follower are You?*

For each of the following questions circle the answer that best applies to you.

Yes No 1. When given an assignment, do you like to have all the details spelled out?

Yes No 2. Do you think that by and large most bosses are bossier than they need to be?

Yes No 3. Is initiative one of your stronger points?

Yes No 4. Do you feel a boss lowers him or herself by "palling around" with subordinates?

Yes No 5. In general, do you prefer working with others to working alone?

Yes No 6. Do you prefer the pleasures of solitude (reading, listening to music) to the social
pleasures of being with others (parties, get-togethers and so on)?

Yes No 7. Do you tend to become strongly attached to the boss you work for?

Yes No 8. Do you tend to offer a helping hand to the newcomers among
your colleagues and co-workers?

Yes No 9. Do you enjoy using your own ideas and ingenuity to solve a work problem?

Yes No 10. Do you prefer the kind of boss who knows all the answers to one who comes
to you for help?

Yes No 11. Do you feel it's okay for your boss to be friendlier with some members of the group than
with others?

Yes No 12. Do you like to assume full responsibility for assignments rather than just to do the
work and leave the responsibility to your boss?

Yes No 13. Do you feel that "mixed" groups--men working with women, for example naturally tend
to have more friction than unmixed ones?

Yes No 14. If you learned your boss was having an affair with his or her secretary, would your
respect for your boss remain undiminished?

Yes No 15. Have you always felt that "he who travels fastest travels alone"?

Yes No 16. Do you agree that a boss who couldn't win loyalty shouldn't be a boss?

Yes No 17. Would you be upset by a colleague whose inability or ineptitude obstructs the work of
your department or company as a whole?

Yes No 18. Do you think boss is a dirty word?

Scoring and Interpretation

To get your score, circle the question numbers 1 through 18 to which you answered yes. Then compare your answers with the groupings below.

A.	1, 4, 7, 10, 13, 16.
B.	2, 5, 8, 11, 14, 17.
C.	3, 6, 9, 12, 15, 18.

If most of your yes answers correspond with Group A, chances are you prefer autocratic leadership. If your total yes answers was highest in Group B, you probably prefer participative leadership. If Group C is one in which you show the most yes answers, you probably prefer free-rein leadership

* Adapted from <u>Mastery of Management</u> by Auren Uris by permission of the Berkeley Publishing Company, (1968).